Is Forgiving a Riddle?

Also by Torry Fountinhead

*The 7 Pillars Your Authentic Self Stands On, Part I of
The Essential Companion Series*

The Beauty, Part of The Contemplation Series

The Soul's Openner, Part II of The Contemplation Series

*Shush! It's a Secret, The Lake Hides His Dummy, Part
of The Rainbow of Life's Secrets*

*Poem: Good Enough, Part of Forever Spoken, The Inter-
national Library of Poetry*

A Tip of an Iceberg Meditations, a series of short books

and many more at work…

Is Forgiving a Riddle?

Part I of "A Tip of an Iceberg Meditations"
Series

By

Torry Fountinhead

Airé Libré Publishing & Computing Ltd.

1st Published as an eBook October 15th 2017
eBook ISBNs:
ISBN-10: 0-9808964-4-4
ISBN-13: 978-0-9808964-4-2

Print Book ISBNs:
ISBN-10: 0-9808964-3-6
ISBN-13: 978-0-9808964-3-5

For more information contact:
Airé Libré Publishing & Computing Ltd.
Suite 306, 185-911 Yates St.
Victoria BC V8V 4Y9 Canada
Tel: 1-250-592-3099.
http://www.al.bc.ca   info@al.bc.ca

Book Web-Site URLs:
http://isforgivingariddle.atipofanicebergmeditations.ca

Part of:
Http://www.atipofanicebergmeditations.ca
Http://www.tipofaniceberg.ca
Http://www.atipofanicebergmeditations.com
Http://www.tipofaniceberg.com

Forgiveness is such a 'tender' gift that I wish, one and all, would recognise that it's already installed within themselves. They may use it immediately, and in every subsequent moment – for the rest of their lives.

In actuality, it's part of our survival mechanism, which allows us to move forward, in a flow rather than in a daze.

I dedicate this book to the whole of Humanity.

VI

Table of Content

"Blessed [is he whose] transgression [is] forgiven, [whose] sin [is] covered."

Psalms {32:1}

x

Is Forgiving a Riddle?

Prologue

Is Forgiving a Riddle?

Well, this is a question, a big one.

The Dictionary mentions 'Forgiving' to originate from Middle English, which is from Old English 'forgifan', from 'for- + gifan' – to give, and in this form it was first used before the 12th century although, the Old English is suspected to start around the 5th century.

Yet, forgiving is already mentioned in ancient texts long before that. The Bible Old Testament already mentioning forgiving in its first book – Genesis {50:17}, as well as many other books within it.

The act, and ability, of forgiving is old and existing from the first moment of Creation, and if we, indeed, are created in the image of God, and God is referred to be the one that can '...forgive us our trespasses...' than we too, are capable of it.

Let us discuss in here, your part of the relationship formula, as it is only you that you may control, change, and choose to renew. The others will benefit, of course, but they would have to do their own inner work.

So let's dive in, for a short time, and ponder the riddle.

Why Forgiving?

Firstly, let us ask why to even entertain the thought, or act, of forgiving. Why would we benefit from it and thus, justify using this *tender gift*.

Since time immemorial, Human-Beings acquainted freedom with flight of birds, the wind's breeze, the flow of a dance movement, and anything else that denoted flow and ease.

Therefore, any cause that may 'shackle' a person down, restricting the person from a free flowing movement, constitutes a limitation.

In these paragraphs, I related to a known physical feeling, but we may feel them too, in much the same way, on an emotional, intellectual, or spiritual level. Therefore, we may also use the 'feelings', as our indicators for any existing limitation, may it be short, or long in duration.

Although limitations have to be identified, not all are without benefit, for example, parents choose to be somewhat limited individuals, for the greater good of their children and the family – they defined the destination, and its benefits and thus, are happy to take part in the journey.

Alas, there are limitations caused by ill-feelings that actually serve no purpose, and bring no real benefit, and certainly undermine the ability of the person to grow and evolve.

Do you recognise the term 'holding a grudge'?

Now, if you are doing the 'holding', what, within you, is not free to flow?

In the spirit of promoting your flow and ease, let's look further at forgiving.

What Forgiving?

Have you ever asked yourself why would you even be in a situation that renders you miserable, so much so, that spontaneously you would 'react' by laying the blame for that situation at the feet of the 'other'?

You may imagine, and see all people walking with their own bundle-of-sticks – all of which are actually yard-sticks that they measure their fellow Humans by. Somehow, people tend to accept similarities, and reject differences. Yes, I'm familiar with the saying that says: 'opposite attract', but this might be initially, at first glance. Do you also know of the saying 'familiarity breeds contempt'?

Where do all these sayings (and many others) come from, if not from experiences people experienced, and decided to remember, as lessons?

Let's assume, you too have such a bundle of yard-sticks, and you're going about your day, all the while (sub-consciously) measuring others. Now comes the main part – if what you see affects you, it will create a feeling within you.

If what measured was to your satisfaction, the feeling will be positive and pleasant. On the other hand, if you got annoyed by it, a *non*-positive feeling would have been created, and the duration of that feeling residing within you, would make a difference to the quality of your life.

One may even look at it from a more scientific angle while, using the metaphor of a trail, becoming a highway, as the same trail is being trodden again and again, so it will happen in our own brain, and its neuron-connectors will be thoroughly created. I do believe that our brain is pliable, that nothing is really cemented in, but we have to recognise it, in order to change it.

Coming back to the necessity of recognition, one must identify the essence of the *non*-positive feeling, and thereafter, trace it back to the origin of the affect.

Once you recognise the affect, and not necessarily the original cause, you've defined the 'what' and thus, ready for the next step.

When Forgiving?

The question of 'when' is entirely depended on the person's level of awareness.

Some people are very tuned to the increase of their feelings' tide. Others, on the other hand, let themselves stew in their feelings longer, and until such time that they really feel the burden-heaviness of it.

Imagine a long-distance jumper focus on the goal of jumping. That goal has two milestones, the one, denoting the short-term goal, and the second, the long-term one. The long-term goal, of course, is the main goal namely, to jump unhindered as far as possible. The short-term goal determines if there is even a chance for that to happen, as it is the bouncing board, and the right stepping on it that will facilitate the long-term goal's happening.

Using this metaphor in our case, we can readily believe that if we pay attention to the immediate change in feeling, we may nip the affect in the bud versus, missing our positive bounce to the next optimal moment in our lives and thus, *not* leaping farther.

Another analogy that we may draw to illustrate the limitations that may be created by the effect on us, is having eye-glasses on, which we may keep touching with unclean fingers, leaving smudge marks on the lenses. Therefore, slowly but surely, what we actually see is distorted by the unclean lenses. Can we trust that what we see then is true?

From my examples, you may conclude that I actually highly believe in being attuned to our feelings, as much as possible, but recognising them as separate from us and thus, utilizing them as the indicators they are.

I also believe in nipping most affects in the bud, as much as we are able to, as a survival mechanism. At the same time, although time is of the essence, one must *not* rush to reaction, as cooler heads always prevail. For example, if your child misbehaves in a manner that might endanger their life, you must respond immediately, as their life is far more important than hurting their feelings. If a colleague at work, on the other hand, is pestering you, you should pause, and find the best way to treat the situation, in such a way that will strive for a win-win result. The pause doesn't have to be long, just enough for converting 'reaction' to 'response', and bring in equilibrium.

This is where we should actually look at what methods are possible to facilitate the forgiving.

How Forgiving?

In order for us to look at how to go about forgiving, we must first look back at the 'affect'.

I'd ask you again to use your imagination, and imagine yourself creating a clay sculpture of you. Clay is not dented very easily, but it does dent, as well as it may become misshapen if the sculptor is not careful.

The sculptor is not the only one that affects the sculpture. The ground it is on should be stable, any movement, and even a good meaning sculptor will mess his sculpture.

If the sculptor is distracted, he would also be distracted from his original idea, he would then have to re-find his focus, re-adjust the unmeant additions, and get back to applying the original vision he had.

The clay in itself might also present a challenge, if its quality is not up to par with the sculptor's vision. I'm not saying that one should not strive to overcome challenging circumstances, I'm just saying that one has to be aware of all that is entailed, before one may proceed in full speed.

Let us say that you, the sculptor, are very clear about the vision for your life, the means available to you for use in achieving it, and the best ways for you to proceed within the circumstances of your current life.

Surely then, it is also clear to you the importance of clearing away any distractions, of which non-positive feelings and grudges, are obviously not serving you.

Let me tell you a very short story of a mare I once ridden, she was a nervous one. A neighbour's cat used to enjoy tormenting her when we were riding in the rink, appearing out of nowhere right at the corner where, the mare was to turn, so when she saw a fast movement from the side of her eye, she would jump, as if a cougar was there, and not a cat. You can easily imagine that it certainly was not comfortable for me, and I did prefer to stay on the horse, and not fly off high in the air.

Well, the cat didn't know that a Human-Being was more responsive than the horse, and the next time we came to the turn, I stopped the mare, turned into the corner, and scared the cat away. The cat definitely looked disappointed at losing the game, but it never came to startle the horse again.

I am trying to illustrate to you two things. The first is the fact that continuous startling of the mare, brought on a nervous disposition – an un-needed attribute to my mind.

The second is that action can be taken to remedy a situation relating to a feeling and an affect and thus, transform the situation and further outcomes, because the actual behaviour would transform too.

In the story with the mare, seeing clearly meant that the mare adjusted her perception, and saw the cat for what it really was, and not a greater threat.

In your case, number of things may be done to achieve the same realization that may transform your perception.

Forgiving, in this sense, is acknowledging what is really going on, changing our attitude towards it, changing our perception of it, taking responsibility for our own choice making – and making a **different** choice.

Before we're going to look at the forgiving techniques, let us look at the question of where the forgiving is to take place.

Where Forgiving?

With relation to 'where', I do not mean to refer to a geographical place although, it, too, should be taken into consideration, but later.

Firstly, the 'where' should denote within you, versus between you and another.

Secondly, and if necessary, it may take place between you and the other.

The other in this case, may be another person, place, an inanimate object, animal, or even God.

The Truth that resides within you is something, whether you know it or not, that would indicate to you whether you are harming yourself or not. It was not a trifle when it was said in the Bible 'Love thy neighbour as thyself'. You do have to love, respect, and treat yourself well before you would know how to do it to another, and then be as loving, respectful and caring towards others in the same way.

Just as an example, a miser is said not to apply this rule, and treat others badly, while thinking of himself only, but if you really examine his situation, you would see that he is not generous towards himself as well.

The reason we have the phrase 'clear conscious' is because we do recognise that in our heart of hearts, we know what is right and what is wrong. We know our transgressions, and we call them shortcomings.

In this light, the difference between virtues and vices, would be the overcoming a shortcoming after recognising it as such. Either by stopping it, or by transforming it, a transformation will create a virtue of it. An example would be a short tempered person would become kind and patient. A selfish person will become considerate. A person using foul language will start giving attention to the words prior to uttering them, and when he'll become a master of his virtue – he would even stop thinking them.

When Socrates, and his predecessors, said 'Know Thyself', they really did indicate that if you take the time for self-investigation, being truthful with yourself, you would achieve a better understanding of yourself. From it, you may derive then an understanding about others, and be better equipped to deal with them, assuming you would wish to do so.

Therefore, firstly, one should look within. Recognise the ties one has to another, where ill feelings exist, and then within one self, let go of them. Like in a tag-of-war, you need two to hold the rope – let go of your side first – save yourself.

This is the choice of having True Freedom, freedom from holding on to any unpleasantness whatsoever.

Thus firstly let go within yourself.

At other times, after you've arrived at the above mentioned conclusions, you might also need to bring peace to the situation between you and the other. Many times an apology would suffice, but sometimes 'agreeing to disagree' might serve just as well.

A side note of interest would be the famous and important Jewish prayer, sung at the eve of Yom Kippur – the Day of Atonement. The 'Kol Nidre' prayer that each person prays individually to God, and nullifying vows, and such, that that same person, within himself, made, God therefore, is the witness and the highest authority within the heart of that person. The person is setting a clean slate to start a new year with, letting go of past vows, which are emotionally based.

You see that I'm actually leading you to the realization that the 'peace within' is fundamental. It is rather impossible to go forth with forgiving, before reaching this inner peace regarding a specific situation.

When you try to establish peace between you and another, opportune moment, place, and privacy should be taken into consideration. The thought in mind should be how to do it in the most gentle and considerate way, as the situation permits, as well as not inducing further non-positive emotions in places, without thought.

Sometimes, it isn't possible to actually get together with the other, so here your wonderful mind may serve as the geographical place of peace. On the screen within your own mind, imagine the two of you conducting a gentle and amiable conversation, and accepting each other's efforts for a better relationship, even if it means saying Goodbyes.

Forgiving Techniques

I mentioned before that the ability to forgive is such a tender gift, actually given and installed within us for the sake of our own survival. It allows us to move forward, in a flow rather than in a daze.

Step out of your hurt, to a higher ground where, you will be able to really see the reasons, occasions, causes, and patterns that led the one who hurt you to do so. You are not your hurt!

Understanding the other party, allows you to acknowledge how you have become part of their story, and what they might perceive as hurt that you have generated in them.

Forgiveness is a balm for your own soul and person therefore, it will be wise to consider that although, things might not seem right, or just, the best way to act is not from non-positive feelings, or grudges, but from a cool, calm, and collected demeanour.

It is a letting-go, lovingly creating a situation, from which you each freely come to your connection.

Decide that health, and peace of mind and heart, are far more important than playing a role in somebody else's story, or cause.

Choose to be free.

Choose to make your own choices – the right

ones though, no self-scarifying please.

All of these to be done inwardly, within yourself

Like the sculptor of yourself, strive to hold the vision for your life in the foreground of your mind and heart. Take into consideration your own circumstances, and understand that over-shooting your abilities undermines both you and others. When the ground of your life is unstable, pause, stable yourself first, before making rush decisions that you might regret later.

Hurts, grudges, non-positive feelings, emotional wounds, traumas, all hold your energy in them. The energy itself is neutral, but where it is held gives it its hue. It is important to release those feelings, so you may release the energy held within them, so you may be able to apply it positively, and become stronger, in mind and soul, in your health, and the will to live.

The releasing may be done inwardly, quietly, and lovingly.

Would you use the metaphor of a caterpillar transforming into a butterfly, to transform yourself from an earth-bound tied-down creature, to one that may soar freely in the air un-shackled?

Would you, within your own mind, surround and wash yourself, and the other party, with a waterfall of a wonderful shining White Light – filling you, washing you, bringing laughter and joy to you both, and your surroundings.

Would you climb the mountain within your imagination, in order to see the whole picture of Life and the situation, rather than just the immediate details that are in the valley below, but then climb down, and aspire to bring peace between you?

Would you love yourself and the other enough to show that peace and joy are the fundamental feeling you would like to have between you?

In all reality, forgiving is like a switch, it has only *on* or *off* options to it. Your decision and determination are the ones that switch it over from the one state to another. Your understanding and willingness just make it easier to perform it.

Understand that this inner work will affect the other, but will not do their inner work for them. Your healing will inspire them, as well as heal whatever you bring into the connection. You cannot, and should not, try and fix or control another. Your domain and mandate is only yourself!

When your ill-feeling overpower you, breathe! And breathe again. Your breath is your connection to your own inner self, and the Life Force, so breathe and calm yourself, first and foremost.

Remember that everything takes time, so have patience.

Count Your Blessings

What is the connection between forgiving and counting our blessings?

Firstly, recognising that we have the power to choose – that we have Free Will, is a fundamental recognition, which initiate the recognition of our blessings, however many or few.

In recognising blessings in our lives, we actually witnessing the fertile ground we're standing on. Thus, we're far more stable, and may become generous.

Generous with our willingness to forgive, to go forth, to grant freedom, as well as have it, and be in a position of power.

All around us, we see everything changing, from weather, to the plant kingdom, the growth of children, to the moods of our loved one (and maybe the not so loved ones), and within us – the change of our feelings, impressions, and thoughts.

Yet, certain things repeat, some daily like the dawn of a new day, the cycles of the moon and the seasons, all of which are part of our blessings, and our participation in it should be our flow. For our flow to happen, we do need to let go of all that unnecessarily may hold us down, like grudges, non-positive feelings etc.

Stopping to take for granted the world, Earth, your environment, yourself, other people, and all there is, will allow us to participate in the dance of Life, to which we need to bring goodwill, and equanimity.

When we recognise the value in all that surrounds us, and all that is with us, and in us, we live in a valuable reality that may then become the fertile ground for a Good Life.

Next, we'll touch the idea of your Freedom, because of it.

Forgiving & Your Freedom

Let's say that you are seeing value all around you, and you're eager to flow forth in your life. Now, test your freedom, test to what actual extent you're able to go forth, and aspire to be better in everything.

Why do I encourage you to test your freedom?

In order to go forth, you do have to have a vision, willingness, perseverance, and focus, but the one indicator that affects your ability to go forth that matters, as it may create an immediate inner stop, will be the state of your feelings.

It is almost like trying to row your boat without any energy to do so, why? because the energy is locked and consumed by your feelings.

Can you imagine a bird trying to fly, by not being so attentive to what it wants to do?

Can you imagine an aeroplane trying to ascend at take-off, with its flaps not extended in the right degree?

Usually, before one forgives, one has 'hurt' feelings. In actuality, these kind of feeling subdue the person, sometimes to the extent of depression, or may make rise to an uncontrolled, and undiscerning anger. Surely it is quite clear that a person in that kind of a state is not free to move forward in a unified fashion?

Unforgiving attitude is like being tied up in ropes, unable to move, and proceed with life.

For a person to be useful in their own life, they must be free. Free to choose, free to move, free to express themselves, free to feel joy, free to invent, and especially - free to dream. By the way, each person, like each type of an aeroplane, comes with their own specifications, and not one way fits all!

There are so many things that may stand in the way of people flowing forth in the lives; surely we shouldn't add an unforgiving nature to it.

Let's choose Freedom.

Forgiving & Response-ability

In continuing from the point that a hurt person might be subdued to one degree or another, the same person might also be able to respond to life, in lesser degree or another.

Therefore, if one measures our ability to respond to life, as one's degree of freedom, the ability to respond climbs high on our list of priorities.

In order to increase our response-ability, there is only one way that will always deliver a positive result, and it is taking a full responsibility to one's life.

In your life, you are always there.

Within the circle of the people in your life, you are always there.

Within the conditions, and or problems, in your life, you are always there.

It becomes quite clear that freedom in your life will enhance your ability to be, or not be, part of them, to whatever degree you choose.

If you follow a premise that you are there, because (either knowingly or unknowingly) you made a choice to be there, even if sometimes it seems unreasonable, e.g., why an abused, but innocent, child would be born to an abusive parent?

The power to say 'NO' is the power to choose whether you're going to continue your presence there, or not.

The question people ask sometimes: why did it happen to me, or why me, only makes a person linger within the hurt. Think of it as driving somewhere, and taking a wrong turn, becoming lost for a short duration of time, having some consequences to it, but stopping – and choosing another direction that will lead you to the right way, and the right path for you.

This is the power of recognising the fact that you are your own person, with your own power to choose, because you took responsibility upon yourself, and your actions.

How else can anyone make any decision whatsoever, if they are not going to exercise their power of choice – their free will?

Even a baby knows if it likes a specific food, or item of clothing, or a toy. How does he know? If not by recognising his own inner self, and tastes.

I'll encourage you to develop a constant responsibility over yourself, and that means anything from the thoughts you entertain to choices, and actions you take. The reason is that you will be able to navigate your own life, and those of whom are dependent on you, in a more of a 'knowing' way, and therefore, a wiser way.

Victim-hood stems from the fear of not exercising self-responsibility, and blame easily follows. Life not being 'fair' is considered as a possibility, instead of looking at life as full of possibilities.

Be not afraid, as we are far stronger than we think we are, and rather be there for one another, valuing one another, than suspecting and doubting – it leads nowhere.

Forgiving Whom?

This question – forgiving whom, is at the core of understanding our own power.

You see, if you do have full responsibility upon yourself, then the first being you must forgive is yourself. Who else got you into the situation that you happen to like, or not like?

Did you hear the saying: 'we are perfect in our imperfection'?

The word perfect can only be applied for something that has reached a point of completion, and therefore, may not apply to us, as we are constantly evolving, changing, and growing, in every aspect of our beings, even our DNA changes, and is not set in stone.

There is another saying that claims that if you give a person a long enough rope – they will be able to hang themselves, but why go so far?

Our worst enemies, critics, doubters, putting-down, etc., are all within ourselves, put there either by us, or by society, parents, teachers, and so on. Isn't it about time that at least those that we've put in ourselves, we will let go of?

The way to do so is to recognise that at every moment of life we can only come from our own best understanding at the time – hindsight is always clearer, but it is in the foresight that we set the tone for a better life.

Therefore, let go of self (or other's) blame, shame, or guilt, stop being your own (and other's) critic, and forgive yourself for anything that made you stray from that which is for your (or yours and other's) highest good.

The forgiving techniques, illustrated earlier, may be used upon yourself too.

The most important method, as the foundation to self-forgiving, is to apply true unconditional self-love, not in a manner of accepting wrong doings, and giving self-justification for them, but calling a spade a spade, understanding where you came from, let go, and proceed in correcting, and evolving in the Right Direction that will encourage your evolution.

At this point, one should also remember that everyone, and everything, is also changing and evolving. For that reason, exercising love, (and preferably unconditional love) upon all, is the right thing to do.

Come from patience, come from forbearance.

Come from love, appreciation, and foresight.

Maybe the people, or situations, are there to highlight to you something that pertains to your own choices, and path. Going away is as much an action as coming forth.

Making a judgement based only on the current few facts, disregarding hidden truths, and or situations, may, unfortunately, mostly lead to misjudging the situation, and therefore, to making wrong choices.

I once witnessed a puzzling occurrence of such judgement and blame, placed wrongly. I witnessed two vehicles, with disability tags on their windshield, entering a small parking lot that happened to have only two disabled parking bays. In the first vehicle there were husband and wife, and in second, a single woman.

The single woman didn't have an immediately apparent disability, for example, a wheelchair, but the man in the first vehicle had a cane.

The man immediately proceeded to shout and blame the single woman for taking up the parking space designated for a 'truly disabled' person, whereby, the woman, who was utterly surprised, commenced to gently and quietly say 'there are some disabilities you cannot see'.

The man proceeded to barrage her with his negative opinions, so the single woman turned to the man's wife, and said: does he count a limiting heart condition a disability? Alas, his wife answered that he really does not care, but at that moment, he suddenly and surprisingly, realised his own wrongdoing, and began apologising.

The single woman turned to him and said: 'don't you know the saying don't judge a book by its cover?'

At which time they both had to 'drop it', let go, be civil, know that now they knew better, and proceed with their own lives.

I am trying to show you that whomever it is you might blame, or disregard, just shows where you are, in understanding, at that moment. You may choose to be open for further considerations, and evolve your understanding at the same time. In this way, you also evolve toward being a kinder person. Not every situation calls for a (guided or misguided) crusader.

Forgiveness starts from within, by accepting yourself, and instead of offering yourself criticism, offer yourself the balm of love, courage to correct the wrong, and or letting go. Thereafter, proceed doing so towards other people – every day.

Consistency with forgiveness is the miracle making of a free person.

If I may, I'd like to recommend two old writings, which may too highlight some aspect of errors in perception, they are If by Rudyard Kipling, and Desiderata, both of which can easily be found to read and consider.

Epilogue

With my intention of addressing Forgiving in a succinct and short manner, I hope I solved some of its puzzle – cleared some of the riddle of it.

A lot more may be said but sometimes all that is needed is highlighting of key points, because our mind is capable of flowing in the right direction (if we just stop distracting it!)

I do believe that Human Beings are capable of Good, Flow, Love, and Gentility if just given the right suggestion. They may rise to heights that even they did not suspect they could.

Our world would have ceased to exist long ago – if it was not so.

Have faith, and be strong and courageous.

A word about this series

In this busy day and age, where people have more input than they sometimes able to concentrate on, I venture to offer a more succinct manner of dealing with subjects of interest, or need.

The image of a tip of an iceberg immediately brings to mind that there is much more unseen, underwater if you may.

Consciousness is very much like the waters of a vast sea whereby, our conscious thoughts are those that exist above the water level, and our submerged portion of the conscious – is very much our unknown part therefore, many times it is called the sub-conscious, or the un-conscious.

Our feelings are just the waves, and wave crests, which are created by the winds of time, and occurrences of life upon the surface.

I'd like to have your brief time of contemplation in reading this short book yet, to impress your mind with a profound message, and content.

It is in the succinct that we may never be overwhelmed, and in overpowering vast amount of input that we are fatigued.

I trust you know that much more could have been said about the subject of the book, but maybe what was said is enough.

I wish you joy and peace – always.

Notes

Notes

Notes

Notes

Notes

Notes

www.ingramcontent.com/pod-product-compliance
Lightning Source LLC
Chambersburg PA
CBHW030814090426
42737CB00010B/1269